Go Outside!

GO CAMPING!

By Peter Finn

Please visit our website, www.garethstevens.com. For a free color catalog of all our high-quality books, call toll free 1-800-542-2595 or fax 1-877-542-2596.

Cataloging-in-Publication Data

Names: Finn, Peter.
Title: Go camping! / Peter Finn.
Description: New York : Gareth Stevens Publishing, 2020. | Series: Go outside! | Includes index.
Identifiers: ISBN 9781538244777 (pbk.) | ISBN 9781538244791 (library bound) | ISBN 9781538244784 (6 pack)
Subjects: LCSH: Camping–Juvenile literature. | Outdoor recreation–Juvenile literature.
Classification: LCC GV191.7 F56 2020 | DDC 796.54–dc23

Published in 2020 by
Gareth Stevens Publishing
111 East 14th Street, Suite 349
New York, NY 10003

Copyright © 2020 Gareth Stevens Publishing

Editor: Therese Shea
Designer: Sarah Liddell

Photo credits: Cover, p. 1 Sergey Novikov/Shutterstock.com; p. 5, 7 wavebreakmedia/Shutterstock.com; p. 9 VP Photo Studio/Shutterstock.com; p. 11 Valentyn Volkov/Shutterstock.com; p. 13 HildeAnna/Shutterstock.com; p. 15 New Africa/Shutterstock.com; pp. 17, 24 (flashlight) Alexander Yakimov/Shutterstock.com; p. 19 Evgeny Karandaev/Shutterstock.com; pp. 21, 24 (sleeping bag) MPH Photos/Shutterstock.com; p. 23 Olesia Bilkei/Shutterstock.com.

All rights reserved. No part of this book may be reproduced in any form without permission in writing from the publisher, except by a reviewer.

Printed in the United States of America

Some of the images in this book illustrate individuals who are models. The depictions do not imply actual situations or events.

CPSIA compliance information: Batch #CW20GS: For further information contact Gareth Stevens, New York, New York at 1-800-542-2595.

Contents

Jake Camps 4
Things to Do 6
Lights Out 16
Camping Is Fun! 22
Words to Know 24
Index 24

My name is Jake.
I love camping!

We hike in the woods.
We pitch the tent.

We go for a nature walk.

We collect sticks.
We make a fire
with them.

We cook food.
I cook a hot dog!

We tell spooky stories!

We put out the fire.
Then, we
use flashlights.

We look at the stars.
We can see so many
out here!

It's time for bed.
We sleep in
sleeping bags.

Camping is fun
for everyone!
Go camping!

Words to Know

flashlight

sleeping bag

Index

fire 10, 16

food 12

nature walk 8

stars 18

stories 14

tent 6